SLOTH
COLORING BOOK
By Logan Parker

Dive into the Wonderful World of Sloth Adventures!

OVER 25 PAGES!

Calling all young artists and sloth enthusiasts! Get ready to embark on an exciting coloring journey with our delightful Sloth Coloring Book for Kids! Explore the magical realm of these lovable creatures and unleash your imagination with every stroke of your favorite colors.

Ignite Your Creativity:
Let your artistic talents soar as you bring these adorable sloths to life. With engaging illustrations and easy-to-color designs, our coloring book encourages children to express their creativity and create their own vibrant sloth-filled masterpieces.